US Navy-

i

Books by Around the World

The Alex Evercrest Series:
The River Front
The Girl on the Grill
Missing
Maggot
Racist
Votive Candles
Windy City
Country Road
Pool of Blood
Sins of the Daughter
Body Parts

The Taelo Series:
Taelo: The Early Years
Taelo: The Golden Feather
Taelo: Journey of Discovery
Taelo: Dangerous Passage
Taelo: Condor Clan Slingers
Taelo: Circumvention
Taelo: The Journey of Sages

A Taelo Story:
The Name of the Child
White Swan and Quiet Pheasant
Broken Spear
Floating Cloud
Quiet Rabbit
Busy Bee
Little Otter& Talking Wren
Burley Bear & Meadow Flower

A Feather-in-the-Wind Story:
The Eastern Elk Clan

Science Fiction Books
The Savitar Series:
Journey's End
Savitar
Confluence
The Problem Solver Series
The Beginning
Drug Lords
Broder Crosser

Single Science Fiction Books:
Current Past and Future
The Door
Event Survivors
The Fold
Viajante 7

Imagination by Courtney Huynh and Chloe Parker

US Navy-A Footprint in My Life
By: *Ron Mueller*

Around the World Publishing LLC
4914 Cooper Road Suite 144
Cincinnati, Ohio 45242-9998

ISBN 13: 978-1-68223-998-8
ISBN 10: 1-68223-998-5

Distributed by Ingram
Cover Picture by: US Naval Command
Cover Design by: Ron Mueller

Ron Mueller

US Navy-A Footprint in My Life

Table of Content

Ron Mueller

Introduction

The Spring rains were making the Mississippi river run high. Spring and my High School graduation were both looming on the horizon. My graduation was the culmination of a high school career that encompassed football, student council and being selected Valedictorian commencement speaker.

My mother, older sister and younger brother were all in Brazil, the country of my birth. They had returned so that my mother could pursue the inheritance of a mountain that her father had bequeathed to her. This would later fall through but she met her next husband on the way there.

I was living with the Perske who had generously taken me in so that I could finish my senior year. They treated me as one of their own and made me feel welcome. Al Perske was into the High School sports scene and his son, Bob, was a quarterback on the team.

I worked part time as a laborer on a construction company while also going to school and playing on the football team and on the wrestling team. The construction work gave me a little money to get by. I was a starter on the football team and mostly played right guard.

I was elected president of the Student Council, I drove a school bus, played football, and wrestled during that last year.

I had a scholarship offer to the University of Arizona based on my wrestling, a scholastic scholarship offer to the University of Iowa and a scholastic scholarship to Dartmouth.

It seemed unreal. I was on the verge of being able to continue my education on my own and had the chance at several top universities. I did not have the means to attend Dartmouth but still there was Iowa and Arizona. I was floating high.

Then reality struck. The University of Iowa wanted my draft number. I did not have a draft number. I was registered with the Brazilian Military. I learned the hard way that any person that lived in the US had to register for the US draft and be given a number. It did not matter what country in the world they were from. They needed a draft number after the age of eighteen.

I was informed that I needed to go to the draft board to get my draft number. The news of the day had made a point that draft dodgers that were apprehended would be immediately conscripted into the Army.

I was turning nineteen and was sure that things would not go well at the draft board office. I did not want to end being drafted into the Army.

There was no one that seemed to be able to give me guidance. I decided to investigate my options on my own.

Airforce, Army, Marines, and Navy all had recruiters that were eager to recruit me. Each had a recruiting story that sounded too good to be true.

I was interested in continuing my education. I visited each of the recruiters and asked them what they could offer me. I had significant offers from all the branches.

It was a hands down win for the Navy with an offer to attend Electronics School, Nuclear Power School, and the Navel Academy Navel Scientific Education Program (NESEP) that would make me an Officer in the Navy. At the time, a career in the Navy was attractive to me.

US Navy-A Footprint in My Life

I arranged with the Navy recruiter to be ready when I went to the draft board office.

I entered the draft board office and was a little surprised by the rather bare large room.

A little old woman was sitting behind a large wooden desk in the center of the room. There was a single chair in front of the desk. I walked to the desk and stood there as she welcomed me and asked for my name and how she might be of help.

"Maybe it would not be so bad," I thought and went on to explain the situation.

She smiled pleasantly and said politely that I was under arrest.

I almost fainted across the desk as my vision collapsed into a tiny, small bright hole. I had my hands on the desk as my vision came slowly back

I asked if she would contact the Navy recruiter that had his office on the same floor. She nodded, smiled, and dialed his number. She called him by his first name and said that she thought she had one for him.

The Navy recruiter came in with the paperwork that he and I had worked through. I walked out of the recruiting office as a recruit in the Navy. I went to boot camp at the US Naval station in north Chicago. It was easy for me to embrace the Navy Motto, "Non sibi sed patriae" or "Not for self but for country."

After completing boot camp, I attended the US Naval Electronics school that was on the same base. In a few months I got certified as an ETR Seaman.

The most significant memory of that time was when toward the end of my schooling, I fell asleep on the beach, got sunburned and had to suffer blisters on my back. The punishment that I faced was to be sent out of the school. I suffered through it and made it to the end.

At its completion I got temporary orders to USS Gunston Hall, in San Diego to await entrance to the Nuclear Reactor Operator School.

This temporary assignment had a huge surprise for me. It was a surprise that lasted a lifetime.

Chapter 1: The USS Gunston Hall

The USS Gunston Hall LSD 5 was named after the plantation home of Statesman George Mason (1725-1792) who played a behind the scenes but important role in the founding of the country. He owned over five thousand acres of land, and he had nine children. He had a view of the Potomac and was able to see the sailing ships that took his goods to Europe.

The USS Gunston Hall was launched in May 1943 and participated in various offensive Pacific actions against the Japanese. It participated in the Luzon, Iwo Jima, and Okinawa offensives.

In 1946 the Gunston Hall participated in the series of Atomic bomb tests labeled "Crossroad."

Then came the Korean war and the Gunston Hall shuttled Marines between Korea and Japan.

A helicopter landing deck was added during that assignment to facilitated nine helicopters to aid in the amphibious assault capabilities.

The next big event was the participation in "Passage to Freedom" that moved eight hundred thousand Vietnamese from the North to the South of Vietnam.

A few years later, the Cuban Missile crisis had the Gunston Hall ferrying Marines through the Suez Canal.

The USS Gunston Hall earned nine battle stars for World War II and another nine battle stars during the Korean War.

Un-beknows to me was that she was about to fulfill her motto, "U CALL WE HALL GUNSTON HALL" and I was going to be on board as she made yet another significant trip to Vietnam.

My arrival was nothing significant. I was on temporary assignment and more or less just added to the Electronics group as another person.

My curiosity and desire to make a contribution had me studying the problems that the Electronics group faced. Everything seemed to be in control, so I spent most of my time in the Electronics shop reading!

The orders to ferry three gun barrels for the USS New Jersey to the Philippines was a surprise to the entire crew.

I wondered why only three barrels until I watched them get loaded. They took up most of the space in the ships dry dock. There was barely enough room for the other crafts also stored there.

I realized that my assignment had taken on a distinctively different path than I had anticipated. At the time I did not realize how significantly different it would be and that it would be a once in a lifetime event.

When the ship sailed out of San Diego it was on its way to Hawaii and then on to the Philippines. The top speed of the Gunston Hall was a whopping five knots (5.75 MPH). The distance to the Philippines was a humongous 7,393 miles. This equated to fifty three and a half days to get to Manila.

I decided to get heavily involved in all the activities that the ship sponsored.

One of the Master Chiefs offered an Aikido class that was held every noon on the Helo deck. During the fifty three days transit of the Pacific, I went from a novice in the class to a red belt.

US Navy-A Footprint in My Life

The Aikido class provided a huge boost to my self-confidence. It taught me the tremendous power that a snap of the hand could have. The Chief emphasized close in self-defense where one was literally up against the opponents chest and with the flick of the wrist could kill.

I had no desire to have that kind of confrontation, but it certainly reduced my fear of facing a belligerent person.

He recommended that I not take the Black belt because then I would be registered as a lethal weapon and libel in any fight I might engage in.

I took his advice.

I looked around at what other activities I could participate in.

Boxing interested me so I signed up for a match.

My opponent was a powerful, broad chested boatswains Mate. I was at the lower end of the weight class, and he was definitely at the top end. I was well built but he had tremendous bulging muscles and a reputation for knocking out his opponents.

I approached the fight with a great deal of apprehension and caution.

I was outscoring him by stepping in and hitting him in the jaw, the ribs and torso and then rapidly stepping away.

It seemed to work very well. And then he hit me in the sternum.

He only hit me once.

Luckily as he hit me, my blow to his nose resulted in a gush of blood and the match was temporarily halted as the nose was attended to.

The world around me was fading into the same wee small hole that I had experienced in the draft board office. The difference was that this time it was very hard to breath and recover.

I was trying not to black out and leaning against the ropes hoping to recover before the match was restarted. For the rest of the match, I danced around and kept my distance from him. He became frustrated with his inability to corner me, and I was able to score a few more points

I won the match.

He congratulated me on giving him his first defeat since he had been on the ship.

I thanked him and I walked away knowing that I would not box again.

Unknown to either of us, he and I would have another significant encounter later in the Philippines.

The arrival to Oahu, Hawaii was graced with an evening sunset that was awe inspiring. I remember standing on the bow watching the evening sun turn the sky from pink to an almost read color. I remembered the saying, "red sun at night sailors delight."

We were only there for a couple of days, and I spent most of my time on the beach. I went to the USS Arizona memorial and viewed the wreckage. It was hard to comprehend that one thousand, one hundred sailors had died and gone down with the ship. It was hard to imagine the carnage that had occurred that day.

Then the longest part of the journey to Manila continued. I concentrated on my Aikido, working on the radar system, and reading.

The Gunston Hall stopped about once a week during the crossing and had what amounted to a picnic and swim session from the platform that was formed when the back of the ship was lowered.

I always took a quick swim but was apprehensive about staying in the water. I had images floating in my head of sharks arriving to enjoy a feast of sailors bobbing in the water.

US Navy-A Footprint in My Life

The arrival at Subic Bay in the Philippines was a great relief in that we got to put our feet on land.

It was enjoyable to walk into Olongapo. Every few buildings was a bar catering to Sailors or Marines. Most of my ship members were soon sitting in a bar drinking.

I and one other sailor friend walked for almost an hour along the street and realized that the entertainment consisted of drinking at a bar of your choice.

When you were entering the bar a young lady would immediately greet you as you entered it. Her job was to convince you to buy her a drink or to take her upstairs.

The line that almost always surfaced was, "I love you no shit, buy me Honda."

I did not really enjoy being constantly asked for a drink or having some rudimentary dialog with someone that I had no interest in, so I was not very interested in the strip just outside of the base.

During the stay in Olongapo and many subsequent port of calls, I hired myself out to stand shore patrol duty. Each ship was required to provide personnel to help police the sailors in Olongapo or any other port of call. Many sailors preferred to go to the bars with their buddies and would pay to have someone take their place on shore patrol.

I was glad to make the extra money.

The Master Chief that had coached me gave me the advice to stand at the end of pay line and collect my money from the sailors that owed me. He commented that once the sailor got away from the pay line the chance for getting the money would quickly vanish.

I took the opportunity to go to the Pagsanjan falls. The trip by bus was long but the reward of taking a canoe ride up the river rapids to the falls was worth the trip. There was a refreshment stand up by the rapids and the opportunity to raft to or to swim in the pool out to the falls.

I chose to swim before eating and went out and enjoyed floating at the base of the falls.

This was where the boxing boson mate and I had our second encounter. I was floating near where the waterfall hit the pool when I heard someone call for help. I turned and saw him sink below the surface and then come struggling to the top. I swam toward him and knew that he would try to grab me. I hit him in the forehead with my open hand and ducked around behind him and grabbed him under the chin and began swimming back to the area where the raft was located. It was lucky that the raft had come out to where we were because I had reached my limit of endurance as I pulled him along. It took several of the people on the raft to pull him out of the water. I stayed in the water and just rested my elbows on the raft as they pulled the it back to the landing area.

The ride back to the ship was uneventful and exhaustion helped me sleep most of the way.tt

Soon after, I took a ferry to Grande Island, swam out to the Chiquita Island, and then swam out away from the beach. I enjoyed the snorkeling and seeing the variety of fish and corral.

It seemed like a great swim, then something stung me. I looked around and it seemed that I was about to be surrounded by a fleet on Man-O-War. I made a hasty retreat but was stung several more times. I crawled out on the beach and collapsed. It took me several moments to realize how close I had come to being stung to death.

I was really concerned about being able to swim to Grande Island but needed to get back to the ship. I had another round of shore patrol that evening.

The Philippines, the people, the time spent swimming all made the arrival and subsequent visits something that I have always enjoyed remembering.

I remember watching what I called giant john boats entering the ship. Two of the boats were twins. They had several fifty caliper machine guns, and several mortars as armament. All three of the boats had multi layered rebar armor covering their sides. The third boat was unique. It had a mortar up front, a huge square tank taking up the center and what I later labeled a Napalm squirt gun at the rear. The tank had the same multilayered shielding as the sides of the boats.

The entire crew learned that the next assignment was to take the Tango boats to Vietnam. Once there it would be the ships duty to take the Tangos to each river mouth along the coast of Vietnam.

It was clear that a new branch of the journey was now unfolding.

I would soon learn first-hand how that affected me personally.

Ron Mueller

Chapter 2: Vietnam

The one week trip to Vietnam was full of defense and offense preparation. Each department on the ship was asked to man a fifty caliber machine gun and to offer up someone to be part of the ship to river mouth transit coverage for the Tango boats.

Training on the fifty calibers and on the transit coverage responsibilities was carried out. I volunteered to be on a fifty caliber at the bow of the ship. This position was just outside of the forward hatch of the sleeping area where I had my bunk and locker.

The area had a sandbag wall with the barrel of the machine gun just above it. Most often I was sitting down and out of view.

I also ended up on the escort landing boat as the fifty caliber gunner. The escort boat accompanied the three Tango boats from the ship to the river mouth. Our duties included providing cover for the boats and if necessary the rescuing of the personnel if the Tango sank.

Much later I was to understand the irony of standing by to save the crew. On almost every trip up the river, one third of the Tango crew lost their lives.

The activity near the DMZ was heavy. The USS New Jersey's booming guns could be heard. It is interesting to know that one shell weighed as much as a VW and could be delivered almost thirty miles inland. The gun barrels that we had delivered was only enough for one turret and the New Jersey had three turrets.

The Australian Navy had several destroyers adding to the coastal bombardment.

I and the crew of the escort craft were almost killed by friendly Australian fire when we decided to take a stroll along the beach after escorting the Tango boats into the river.

We were walking cautiously along the beach when we were almost knocked on our butts by the impact of an explosion ahead of us. We ran like the wind back to our landing craft and pulled the craft back off the beach. Our radio man was frantically calling in to have the shelling stop.

The river clearing routine was a continuous round robin of going down along the coast, "opening up the river," sending the bodies of the Tango boat crew off the ship, proceeding to the next river, and then going back to the DMZ and repeating the cycle.

I don't recall how often we made that circle.

I had a rude awakening about the fact that the "volunteers" that made up the crews of the Tango boats were clearly on the insane side. Two incidents made this very clear.

One was when on an early Sunday morning I was sitting in the ships mess hall reading. Sitting several tables away was a crew member of one of the Tango boats. He would periodically chuckle as he flipped the pages of a photo album.

He looked over at me and said he wanted to share some of his pictures.

I walked over and he began to show me some of his pictures.

It would be an understatement to say I was shocked.

One photo had him holding a headless baby. He had a caption below the picture saying, "look Ma, no head." I wondered who had taken the picture.

Another picture had a young woman in flames running toward him. The caption below the picture, "the women here are hot mama's."

I thanked him for sharing and quickly returned to my book, but reading was out of the question.

Another incident happened to a mess cook that was taking the garbage to dump over the back of the boat. The banging of the trash can triggered one of the Tango crew members who almost beat the mess cook to death. The young mess cook was air lifted to a nearby hospital ship. There was no action taken on the attacker. I believe a few rivers later; he was one of the fatalities.

It was clear that all the members of the tango boats were all beyond the normal. Much later when I was in the Bremerton Naval hospital to have surgery on my ankle, I visited the insane ward of the hospital. I learned then that the Tango boat crew members were well beyond any of those at the hospital. It was clear then that the Tango boat assignment was a way to eliminate those individuals that were beyond what the military doctors thought they would know how to handle.

It also became clear to me why those individuals were from every military branch and of every profession in the military. The qualifying criteria was to be extremely crazy.

This realization has stuck with me throughout the years and ever conflict generates individuals that lose their mental way.

I don't remember the exact rotation back to the Philippines but there were several.

In the Philippines, I spent most of my time standing shore patrol to make additional money or going out to the beach.

One event that stands out to this day was walking the shore patrol circuit with a shipmate that was half my size. We both were pulled into a bar where a major fight was underway. We announced our presence and called for the fighting to stop. One huge sailor turned and came in on the attack. I was sure that the both of us were in for a beating.

US Navy-A Footprint in My Life

My partner pushed me slightly aside leaped forward and delivered a kick to the on rusher that caught him under the chin and caused him to fly back, hit the wall and fall to the floor. He was out.

The room went quiet.

The local shore patrol entered and took over. The two of us were asked to return to the base and report to the person in charge of the shore patrol. Both he and I were interrogated about the incident. Since I had not been in the fight, I was dismissed. I waited for my partner to be dismissed because he had additional interrogation to go through. It turned out he was a black belt in Karate. He was notified that he would never be allowed to stand shore patrol again, but he was dismissed, and charges were not brought against him.

I let my Master Chief know about the incident and learned that the shore patrol officer had been very generous not to write my partner up for a Captain's mast. That would have been like standing before a judge to be sentenced for breaking the law.

It seemed like the river clearing time was going to extend forever but in reality it ended in about six months.

On one of cycles, the ship went up the Mekong river and landed in Saigon, now Ho Chi Minh City. I had little interest in spending time in a very crowded city.

I focused on making money and stood watch almost the whole time.

The main memory I have of that upriver trip was the floating plants coming down river, the many boats that had people living on them and the many boats that were floating markets.

It represented a very different and seemingly alien way of living.

A recreation stop in Vũng Tàu provided me a view of Vietnam that I still recall today. I am not sure where along the beach the military had established their area, but it was limited to military personnel and their guests. It had palm trees a little grass and an inspiring view both out to sea and inland.

I enjoyed several days there swimming in the clear water. I was surprised that barbed wire had been dropped in the waters on each end of the beach to prevent access.

One of the attractions was the fact that you could get a full meal with grilled steak, fish, and sausage free of charge.

It fit my income of only a few hundred dollars a month.

I don't recall what was done with that Tango boats, but I believe they were left in the Philippines to get repaired.

I wonder to this day how many more young men were sent on their way to the next world as part of their Tango with death.

The journey home would have its own additional challenges, but it would also show me another part of Asia that I would later in life visit often.

In Hong Kong, I spent some of the money that I had made. I bought a carved wooden water buffalo that I still have to this day. It currently resides in the basement.

US Navy-A Footprint in My Life

I took a trip by bus to look over the border into "Red China." It was a thrill to see into the land of the powerful giant north of Vietnam. Little did I know that I would travel much of China in my next life as an engineer for Procter and Gamble.

One of the memories I have was of a dinner sponsored by the Captain of the Gunston Hall. He sat at the rotating table with me and explained all the food that was brought out. He also taught me how to use chopsticks.

The food was great. We also watched an on stage performance which I do not recall but it made the two hours at the table go by smoothly and enjoyably.

I did suffer an injury. The next day, I could barely use my right hand because it was sore from using chopsticks.

I spent another sum on buying a set of Noritake table ware most of which is still in one piece.

The next stop that I recall was in Sasebo, Japan. I did not get any sightseeing in but once again had a memorable incident during my shore patrol duty.

I don't recall why I was walking up the street by myself. My defensive weapon was a nightstick. It was daylight and I was not anticipating any significant activity.

Suddenly a crowd chasing a sailor holding his hat in one hand came running toward me. It was clear that he was not going to outrun the crowd.

I pushed him into a recessed doorway and stepped in front of him and was quickly surrounded by the angry crowd. Lucky for me they stopped and in broken English, one of them told me that I should give the sailor to them because he had mistreated one of the bar girls.

I saw a shore patrol vehicle coming up the narrow street and then it honked its horn and the open anger of the crowd seemed to dissipate. They began to disperse but continued to demand the sailor.

I was happy to turn the sailor over to the regular shore patrol. I continued my patrol as they took the sailor back to the base.

Several of the crowd walked with me for a short time and the rest of my patrol was uneventful with the exception that I had to write a report about the incident.

Then it was time to make the trip back to San Diego. Our ship, the slowest of the fleet returning was put at the head of the convoy. All the other ships were in formation behind us.

Then a monsoon hit. Huge waves swept over the ship repeatedly hitting the conning tower.

The faster ships broke free from the formation and headed back to San Diego at speeds that for most of them was at least triple the speed of the Gunston Hall.

The power of the storm was apparent by the fact that the right gun mount had its barrel pointing forty five degrees into the air and the deck it was on was ripped at its forward edge.

We spent the next forty some days slogging along and enjoying our time at sea.

Chapter 3: Nuclear Power School

The return from Vietnam was a revelation. The relatives of many of the sailors were on the pier to welcome them home but in general the public was very negative about the activities going on in Vietnam. The signs in many homes in the area were, "dogs and sailors stay off the grass." There was no warm welcome.

Shortly after returning, I was given my orders transferring me to San Francisco to attend the first half of the Nuclear Power school. This was the Math and science phase. It was an intense eight hours a day with a full two days of weekend homework training.

I was given quarters on the base but also had the option of living off base. Off base, a few of my classmates and I rented an apartment in Vallejo. We each assumed part of the work to keep our apartment clean. My role was to cook the few meals that we ate there, which was mostly on weekends.

The only thing that I really recall about living there was that there was a fig tree that provided delicious figs for the entire time that I lived there. It seemed that I was the only one that knew what they were, so I always had a good supply of figs.

I also had an assigned on base room where I spend quite a bit of time doing homework during the day. I had a roommate assigned to the same room.

One day I came into the room to find a coffee can full of marijuana. I immediately flushed it down the toilet. The roommate came in a little later and got really mad. I reminded him that it was my duty to turn him in for doing drugs. He calmed down. I made it clear that if he ever brought drugs into the room again, I would turn him in.

Upon completing the first phase of Nuclear power training we all received transfer orders to the US Naval Nuclear Power facility in Idaho. As part of the completion ceremony, we were asked to turn in any persons that we were aware of using drugs and that failure to do so would result in getting kicked out of the program. I kept quiet hoping the on base roommate would do so as well.

It was at this point that I learned that the roommate that was smoking pot was detained and was not going to Idaho. Later I learned he got a general discharge that booted him out of the Navy but was not a dishonorable discharge. He stopped by in Idaho and shared how happy he was to get out.

US Navy-A Footprint in My Life

Pocatello and Idaho Falls were two small cities where most of the Navy personnel lived. I and three other trainees shared a house in Idaho Falls where we each had our own rooms. The nuclear power training facilities were located about an hour away and each morning we would all get on a bus and ride out to the training site. The ride was across the barren desert that was populated by a host of jack rabbits. To this day I am convinced that the bus was the rabbit's worst nightmare. At night, the rabbits would come out to the highway to enjoy the warm black top and in the early morning around five the buss would come along and run over them. The continuous thump, thump, thumping was a distraction to most of us trying to get a few more winks during the ride.

The operational training was again an intense, eight hours a day, activity. It consisted of memorizing the layout of the entire nuclear power facility. Every motor, pump, valve, pipe size and length, the height of the motor mounting pads, the position and reading range of every meter and the motion the operator went through for every imaginable situation had to be memorized. Each day had a certain amount that had to be done. If you did not score one hundred for the day, you stayed an extra two hours to get the necessary score to get on the bus back to Idaho Falls. I thought that the theoretical phase had been intense until my experience at the reactor site.

The nice feature of the assignment was that the site was run on the southern swing shift where there was a four day weekend every month. This meant some longer weeks, but the four day weekend allowed for a great time snow skiing in the winter and in the spring fishing and exploring the mountains and doing a variety of other outdoor activities.

On one such activity a roommate and I went for a ride in his light blue convertible Datsun. We drove along a mountain logging road a that descended down a steep slope into a small valley that had several operational beaver dams. It was a scenic enjoyable ride where we saw beavers working on their dams, deer grazing and got a glance of a bear walking along one of the ponds created by the beavers.

About noon we turned to drive back the way we had come in thinking we would stop at some small restaurant. The drive back up the mountain seemed to be going ok until as we began to climb back up the steep hill the engine coughed a couple of times and died. I got out and checked what was going on. It turned out the SU carburetors were not able to provide the necessary fuel to the engine because of the steep angle we were driving up.

My buddy and I tried to push the car up but soon it was clear we were not going to be able to get to the top. The sun was near setting when I suggested we set up camp and get ready to spend the night.

US Navy-A Footprint in My Life

We had not come prepared to camp out. Luckily, he had his sleeping bag in the trunk. We found a place under a pine tree that had a good layer of pine needles that we pushed together to make our mattress and then we opened the sleeping bag and used it to provide a cover. It was a long cold night with only a few hours of sleep until we were happy to be awakened by the morning sun.

By this time were knew we were in trouble because walking out would take at least another day. We tried again to push the car up the mountain, but it was clear we were not going to make it. We were just starting to hike out when we saw a rider on a horse approaching. We pointed down to the car and explained the problem we had.

He smiled and said he had a deal for us. He would pull the car to the top of the hill but then in return we would have to work for the day and help to separate two large sheep herds that had got mixed together.

We took him up on the deal. We pushed and he pulled, and the car easily was pulled up to the top. We got in, the car started, and we followed him to his campsite where he had a wagon where he slept. He made us a nice fried egg and lamb meat breakfast and afterwards gave each of us a can of peaches to top it off.

We then followed him to an area where the separating activity was to take place. He explained the process. I was put in the middle and told how to recognize the markings of the two sheep herds and how to move each sheep in the right direction. It was me in the middle working with several dogs that once I moved the sheep in the right direction the dogs would take over and keep the sheep going in that direction.

The shoes I had on put a blister on my foot, so I chose to take them off and put them to the side. For most of the day I was barefooted and walked through sheep dung. This was of great amusement to the herders who each took their turn to tease me.

But we were both well fed. Lunch was again lamb, beans, and a piece of bread but as I recall we were hungry enough to think that once again we had a meal fit for a king.

The day ended with the two sheep herds each going there own way and a thank you for the help from the herders.

We arrived back at our apartment exhausted but happy about our drive.

There are several memories of my hunting experiences in Idaho. One was about hiking down into a valley from the top of a mountain to hunt for Elk. Another was the day that I gave up hunting.

Let me begin with the preparation that I went through to take up elk hunting.

I had hunted when I lived in Iowa. I had often hunted squirrel, pheasant, and raccoon.

US Navy-A Footprint in My Life

I had learned to handle guns and generally enjoyed the hunt. I had used a twelve and twenty gauge shotgun, an over and under twenty two long rifle gauge and twenty gauge shot gun and had used a twenty two gauge pistol to shoot the racoon out of the tree that the hunting dogs had treed. Hunting had been one of the activities that I had often participated with my stepdad.

Elk hunting was different in that a more powerful rifle was required and the range for a shot was much farther.

I purchase a used 308 and practiced shooting it out in the desert. It took me some time to get used to the longer distance for the shots, the drop the bullet had over that distance and the kick delivered by pulling the trigger. The rifle had a scope which was another feature I had to get used to.

All of my room mates were into the hunting scene, so we planned several hunting outings. We would go out in the early morning before sunrise, set up a line across a small valley and then march along prepared to flush out an elk.

On one of our first hunts, we returned empty handed to the car. We were all freezing and decided to get in and go to a restaurant to get breakfast. I was putting our rifles into the car, barrels pointed to the floorboard when one of the rifles fired. The floor mat disappeared! The bullet had pulled it through the hole it had created. It was my 308 that had gone off.

I took the 308 to the gunsmith who informed me that the trigger had been filed so that it would fire with just a touch. He replaced the mechanism so that it would function as intended.

That experience had all of us totally emptying our weapons before putting them into the car.

I did repair my friend car floorboard.

One of the guys shot an Elk and we had enough Elk meat to last all of us for the entire class period. We had the Elk butchered by a local meat shop who kept our meat for us and who took a part of the Elk as payment. This arrangement suited us and allowed us to continue to hunt knowing that the butcher would take the meat.

We planned one trip to an area where a gold mine had once operated. We drove to a parking spot that was near a mountain top fire tower look out and hiked down the trail into the valley. It was a challenging walk down and I began to worry about getting an Elk back up to the car.

About two thirds of the way down we encountered the abandoned mine. A small, clear cold water stream ran by the mine and went down into the valley. It was time for lunch. In the past, rabbits and squirrels we abundant so we had agreed to minimizing our load because we expected to bag our lunch and dinner. I had only brought a pan to cook in, a couple of onions, some oil, salt, and pepper.

US Navy-A Footprint in My Life

I built a fire ring and put a pot of water on. I asked the group to see if they could get a rabbit or squirrel. One of the team who was a top marksman saw a red squirrel. He pulled his handgun out and shot off its head. I cleaned the little squirrel and put it in the pot. It soon disappeared. It gave the water a good flavor but was hardly sufficient to quench our hunger.

We were all hoping to get an Elk on which to feast. The next day proved to be even worse, no Elk, no rabbit, no squirrel. It was a water, onion, oil, and salt soup. I threw in a few greens that were growing along the small stream.

I suggested we hike up a trail shown on the map that went around and over the mine location back to the parking lot.

Everyone agreed that it was time to get out.

It was an exhausting hike. About halfway there we came upon a branch in the trail. We stopped to rest. The discussion was about abandoning the rifles and other stuff. I said I was planning to carry up what I had carried down.

I had kept secret that I had a candy bar for each person for such an emergency. My buddies at first accused me of having a stash for myself. I let them know that I had kept it for an emergency and if they were going to object, I would eat all the bars myself. They all relented and thanked me, but they were still planning to drop their stuff.

It was at this point that a rider on a horse rode toward us from the branch in the trail that let away from where we were going.

He asked if we were all OK. My buddies began to say that they were.

I stepped in and said that we needed help and could he take my buddies rifles and backpacks. He agreed and told us how to get to his camp.

I thanked him. I kept my stuff because I knew that I would make it to my car. One of my buddies commented that he would probably never see his stuff again.

The hike continued up the mountain side. As we approached the parking lot the trail narrowed and provided a dramatic view of the valley that we had all just hike up from. The early morning sun's rays was streaming down illuminating the forest and valley. it seemed that it was letting us know that we had made it.

One of the guys had a camera and I asked him to take a picture.

We all got into the cars, and I led the way to the campsite location that the horse rider had described. He was back and had piled our stuff to the side of his camp. He was out with his wife and family and their horses.

We thanked him for the help and then after a brief conversation we all got into the cars with the intention of immediately going to the restaurant that he had suggested to us.

US Navy-A Footprint in My Life

We entered the restaurant put in our orders and were talking about our adventure. I commented that we would be able to tell our stories to our kids and grandkids and show them the picture of the valley that John had taken.

John shook his head and replied that he had been too tired to take the picture.

It was toward the end of the hunting season when I experienced the event that ended my hunting career. I was the very last person at the top of the valley hill side as we walked along. I had just climbed over a large fallen tree and sat down. I was taking in the sun rays streaming through the clouds when a huge elk with an amazing set of antlers walked out of the trees toward me. He was followed by a female elk. They both stopped and looked at me.

I was sitting with my rifle on my lap. I took in the sun streaming down. The beauty of the two animals and knew that I was being given a message from above.

I smiled and told the Elk that it was his lucky day and that I had just ended my hunting days.

My buddies were shouting out that a huge elk was coming my way. I lied and said that I had not seen it.

It was the last day that I hunted.

I also did a ton of fishing along the varies small streams descending from the mountain sides. There was one trip that I remember. I was hiking downstream and came to a favorable flat area by the stream that I thought would make a good camp. I put up my one person tent.

I had not packed any food.

Made a fire ring were I could use my cast iron frying pan and then went out to do a little fishing.

I caught two trout in rapid succession. It was as if they had never seen a lure. A little butter, a little salt and a sizzling pan got the fish ready. Then a fork to eat with was all that was needed.

After cleaning everything up, I climbed into my sleeping bag.

The next morning was a repeat of the evening before and after breakfast I hiked back to the car.

Then it happened. An announcement meeting was held in the warehouse at the training site. Once it was over, I turned to walk out. I was walking toward the exit when out of the corner of my eye I saw this huge steel ladder that you would put on the side of a water tank falling toward me. I stepped back but the end of the ladder hit my right ankle. I went down. I was taken to the hospital where they wrapped it in a compression bandage and then a cast. I continued the training and qualified, but my medical condition needed to be resolved.

Chapter 4: Bremerton

Puget Sound Naval Shipyard is a United States Navy shipyard covering 179 acres on Puget Sound at Bremerton, Washington and has been in uninterrupted use since its establishment in 1891. Seattle is across Puget Sound to the east.

The entire region is an area that has the ocean water, the surrounding mountains that often pierce through the clouds to be graced by the sunshine above. It was an area that I fell in love with.

I received orders to a non-nuclear powered ship to be a part of a shake down crew for the USS Coronado as it went through some refurbishing. It was in port in Bremerton, Washington.

On arrival, I was assigned the duty of checking out the new radar system and bringing it on-line. I discovered that the main power unit was defective. When I reported this to the officer that I worked for, he did not believe me and asked me to check it again. I did and reported the problem again. He still did not believe me and asked me to get help from the shore support unit.

Two Master Chief radar specialists came out and agreed with my findings. The officer in charge argued with them until one of the Master Chief asked why he was arguing with them and said they were returning to their shop.

Once they had left I was the target of his ire. I later learned that he had already signed for the system as having been tested before I arrived, and he was going to face the negative feedback because the failed unit cost tens of thousands of dollars.

Not long after the Coronado left for its new homeport at Norfolk, Virginia.

I left for the Bremerton hospital for surgery on my ankle.

I was relieved to be going to the hospital and I thought that I was done with the assignment to the Coronado, but this was not to be.

The surgery was to remove a bone chip on the inside of my right ankle. I was in a hospital ward with beds down each side of the ward like you see in the movies. There were something like ten beds on each side of the ward and two rooms at the very end that were reserved for the very badly wounded.

There were two sailors who had interesting stories in the beds adjacent to me.

One had been tuning up his large Harley motorcycle. He had it up on two cement blocks as he worked on it. He was gunning the throttle as he adjusted the tuning when he accidently bumped the shifter and the bike lunged forward, hit the power pole immediately in front of it and flipped back on top of him and broke his leg.

The second had a more interesting story about going for a ride on his Honda motorcycle. As he left his house, a bird hit him on the shoulder and made him stop until the pain subsided. He went on and then a fox ran out in front of him, and he slid to the side of the road but was OK. He continued his ride and as he zoomed along through the forest a deer ran out in front of him. When he hit the deer he flew over it and went sliding face down to the highway. He was wearing a helmet and a full leather outfit, gloves, and heavy duty boots. He stopped sliding as his nose started being scraped by the pavement. His elbows and hands were all abraded. The boots tips had ground down to expose his toes. He had a broken collar bone, a broken leg and abrasion wounds on the tip of his nose, his elbows and hands, the tip of his toes and one knee.

A forest ranger arrived on the scene and called in the accident. He asked what he should do about the bike and the deer.

The sailor said that he gave the ranger the bike and the deer because he understood the message from above and that he would never ride a motorcycle again.

The two rooms at the back to either side of the nurses station had two badly wounded soldiers. One had lost his arm and most of his legs. The other had lost all limbs and was badly burned. He was constantly crying out for someone to shoot him a get him out of his misery.

It was hard to stay in the ward. I was lucky in that I had been issued crutches and could leave the ward.

I spent most of my time exploring the hospital. It was on one of my explorations when I went to the floor where the mentally ill were treated that I learned how really mentally gone the young men on the Tango Boats were. The patients at Bremerton were what I call sane. I got out of the wing as soon as I could because at that time I would probably have qualified to be in that wing.

In my exploration I ran into a couple that ran a charter fishing boat. They had a standing offer to take two sailors out when they had the room. I immediately volunteered.

I don't remember where they had their charter boat anchored but it was only a short distance to the Pacific coast. They took me on board and showed me how to fish for salmon. I did that and while doing that I helped several of the paying customers. They thanked me and invited me back again as one of their deck hands. Still on crutches, I went out with them as often as I could.

US Navy-A Footprint in My Life

What was interesting was that I would trade a whole salmon that I had caught for a quarter of a smoked salmon that a person on the pier offered. It was a great exchange because I could snack on the smoked salmon but could not keep a fresh fish. I often left the fresh fish with my hosts.

My hospital stay came to an end and I received my orders sending me back to the USS Coronado. I was greatly disappointed or should I say depressing.

Shortly after my return, the officer that I worked for informed me that he was assigning me to be one of the ship's policing patrol that was responsible to patrol all the decks of the ship.

I informed him that my ankle could not take that kind of heavy wear so soon after my surgery.

He let me know that it was an order and that I would comply or get written up for disobeying a direct order.

His attitude infuriated me. I complied but was looking for a way to get off the ship.

Then I saw a message from Admiral Zumwalt asking for volunteers to be on the USS Tucumcari PGH2 and that volunteers should be sent to get an interview at the Tucumcari's recruiting office.

I took the message to my officer in charge. He said that he would not allow me to volunteer. This surprised me since he was breaking an order from an Admiral.

I chose to take a chance during my lunch time. I walked up the pier to the recruiting office for the interview. During the interview, I explained the situation that I faced with the officer that I worked for and that if I was selected, I would need help in getting off the ship.

The senior recruiting officer replied that I was accepted. He walked back to the ship with me. He instructed me to get my things together and meet him back at that ships watch station with all my belongings. He would visit with the Captain and with the officer I worked for and let them know that I was now a member of the USS Tucumcari.

To say I was elated would be an understatement. What a way to escape the USS Coronado.

Chapter 5: USS Tucumcari

The USS Tucumcari (PGH-2) was a Boeing-built hydrofoil. It was named after Tucumcari, New Mexico. The Tucumcari was one of two prototype hydrofoils contracted by the Navy for the purpose of evaluating the latest hydrofoil technology. The waterjet propelled Patrol Gunboat Hydrofoil Tucumcari (PGH-2) was built for the Navy at a cost of $4 million in Tacoma, Washington, and then assembled and outfitted at a Boeing facility in Seattle. The Tucumcari, an extremely fast, highly maneuverable, prototype hydrofoil gunboat designed to perform well even in heavy weather, represented the culmination of 10 years of hydrofoil development. It was the winner in the hydrofoil technology.

The Tucumcari was transferred to the Atlantic Fleet in August 1970. After operating off the east coast until 1971,

The Tucumcari was deployed to northern Europe and to the Mediterranean to demonstrate the capability of hydrofoil water jet propulsion to other NATO nations. It was hoped that the demonstration would stimulate the development and production of a NATO guided missile hydrofoil fleet.

The Tucumcari had one forward wing and two wings at the back part of the ship.

The adventure for me began almost immediately as the Tucumcari flew alongside the Chesapeake Bay Bridge racing the cars that were crossing. We were training in preparation for a series of demonstrations that would take us from the North Sea to the entrance of the Black Sea.

I was assigned the duty of maintaining the electronics that controlled almost all aspects of the Tucumcari. My specialty was radar which the Tucumcari had. The control system for the hydrofoil wings, the bow doors and the navigation controls were very sophisticated for the time, and I received individual instructions from several Boing personnel. I qualified on all the systems.

The other role I played was as navigator. This utilized the radar and Loran signal that was beamed from ground based stations. I would take the loran readings and plot the location on the coastal map. I used the radar system and any unique coastal feature to verify the Tucumcari's exact location at each point of time.

US Navy-A Footprint in My Life

Since it was expected that the Tucumcari would often fly throughout the day and night, navigation was a duty that the three of us shared. We also shared being at the helm and flying the boat.

The Tucumcari rode piggyback across the Atlantic on the deck of the USS Wood County arrived to Copenhagen, Denmark and off loaded the Tucumcari from the deck of the USS Wood County that was accompanying the Tucumcari on its tour of Europe. We hit a storm where several of us went out to check and tighten the cables holding the Tucumcari down. Had it not been for the personal safety lines one of us would most likely have been washed overboard by the waves that were hitting the Wood County.

The Tucumcari and Wood County visited seven NATO nations and 16 ports

In Demark, the ports were Copenhagen and Frederikshavn.

In Germany, the ports were Kiel and Olpenitz.

After a transit across the North Sea there was a stop at Rosyth, Scotland.

Then we flew to the Isle of Portland and Portsmouth in England.

Then it was a return to the European mainland at Brest and Toulon, France.

Then the Tucumcari went through the straights of Gibraltar into the Mediterranean. We had ports of call in Naples, Brindisi, La Spezia, Italy.

Then we went on to Greece to the cities of Augusta, Sicily, and Athens.

The final port was in Gölcük, Turkey.

For me it was an adventure that is hard to forget. We operated with the navies of each of the NATO countries and visited the other ports of call to give rides to dignitaries and their families.

One of the very first activities was to work with the Danish navy to determine if they could set their ocean mine sensitivity to be able to counter the thread of hydrofoils. They had set up a series of tests that had the Tucumcari flying over their mine. They kept adjusting the sensitivity of the mine to the point that the mine were exploding after we flew over them. After many flights over the mines the setting got sensitive enough that it would explode but long after the Tucumcari had past it. The adjustments continued until the explosion lifted the back of the Tucumcari and it rode out on the wave created by the explosion. The technicians called us up and said they thought they had it and asked if we would like to take one more pass over a mine.

Our Captain thanked them for the invitation and suggested that instead they all gather at the officers club for a round of drinks.

US Navy-A Footprint in My Life

I was into bicycle riding and had purchased a bicycle and enjoyed a ride almost every day.

There was one weekend ride that I went on that remains clearly in my mind. I was riding along a country road with no special goal in mind. I stopped a local pub that was situated out in the countryside. I had a beer and a sandwich. I became somewhat of a celebrity when they found out I was an American sailor. No one spoke English but there was one young girl that was learning it in school. They brought her into the pub, and she became an interpreter as several men and women asked me questions. It was a fun lunch conversation.

After lunch I continued my ride. Then up ahead I saw a beautiful yellow landscape. The fields were planted with mustard plants that were blooming. I petalled along until I began sneezing. I sneezed so long and hard that I could not ride my bicycle. I turned around and sneezed my way out of the field to a point where I could get back on my bicycle and ride away. Beautiful mustard fields but allergy deadly.

My other memory was of going across to Malmo, Sweden. At that time, the transit was by ferry. I got on in the morning, enjoyed the ride across, and had a late meal. I am not sure the exact time of day but after spending some time riding around in Sweden, I boarded the ferry and rode back.

We participated in several naval exercises to demonstrate the capability of the Tucumcari. We were clearly the most maneuverable and capable of the fast attack speed boats.

We also took many naval officers, wives, and children out for hydrofoil rides.

One of the goals was to see if we could tune in the foil control system to the shape of the North Sea waves. I had been doing some adjustments to improve the performance. We went out in a very significant storm and learned that the North Sea had its own surprise for the Tucumcari.

A wave swept over us, and the Tucumcari hit the next wave head on. The force of the water peeled the bow doors back like two banana peels. I rushed out and tied each door off so that we would not lose them. The captain commended me but told me he thought I was a little crazy to go out to tie the doors to the side of the boat in the middle of the storm.

We hobbled back to port and then scheduled the repair of the two doors. I had the doors modified so that I could pin the two halves of the door together to provide extra protection from waves hitting the bow. The pin could be put in and removed by hanging down from above.

Another problem that I solved was the fact that the front hydrofoil hydraulic cylinder control wiring would short out and we would lose control of the front foil. Several solutions dealing with the wiring and connectors were tried but we kept having that problem. My solution was to pack the chamber that housed the hydraulic system with heavy duty grease to keep out the water. This grease was super thick and when packed into the chamber it provided the protection that the system needed.

I got his done but had spent almost two consecutive days without sleep doing this because we were slated to continue the journey and fly down the English Channel. We normally berthed on the Wood County but because of the Transit, the Wood County went on ahead to and the Tucumcari stayed overnight in Copenhagen.

We left in the early hours of the next day. I slept during the departure until it was time to take my navigation watch.

The startling surprise that I was to walk in on was one that tested the person on the helm and put fear in all of our hearts.

Ron Mueller

Chapter 6: Scotland, England, France

I think I slept the entire time it took to leave Copenhagen and get to Rosyth Scotland located just north of Edinburgh. The distance between the two is approximately six hundred miles or roughly six hundred miles.

The activities at Rosyth was the beginning of what I thought of as the "Joy Ride" phase of the trip. Every day we would make a series of trips out along the Firth of Furth toward the North Sea. We were dressed in our best uniforms and hosted the families of various dignitaries and senior military officers. This was a routine that would go on at every subsequent port of call.

While in Rosyth, I bicycled the countryside and found the hills very challenging and soon was looking for easier things to do. A tour of Edinburgh was certainly of interest but now I only recall a few Cathedrals and don't recall the few pubs I did visit.

We stayed in Rosyth for a few days and then began the transit to Portsmouth, England. During the flight down the English Channel to Portsmouth, England we almost lost our lives.

We Flew out of Rosyth while the morning was still dark. I was asleep getting ready for my navigation duties the next morning. I woke up early, decided against a cup of coffee and went up to the con. I looked over the shoulder of the person doing the navigation, at the radar screen and saw a green line across it in front of the Tucumcari. I immediately shouted out to the helmsman to take a hard turn to port.

The person at the helm heeded my order. Through the fog an oil pipeline running back to shore from a drilling platform made its appearance. The Tucumcari literally skidded through the turn on one back wing and half of the front wing. I know the Boing folks, who had designed the Tucumcari would have been proud to learn that the center of gravity maintained its designed location of going through the center of the boat even as it had water coming up onto the port deck as it executed the skidding turn.

Had I stopped for my morning cup of coffee, we would have hit the pipeline and that would have ended the Tucumcari and probably killed most of the crew.

I immediately sent the person who had been navigating below. Our skipper was almost instantly at the con asking what had the H--- had just happened. He said that from that point forward the person that I had relieved would not be standing the watch by himself and that one of us had to monitor his accuracy.

That person had the Tucumcari flying dangerously close to shore. I adjusted the course and put the flight path down the middle of the channel. We reached Portsmouth a few hours later with no additional issues.

We came to the realization that the person that almost killed us was not qualified to navigate by himself. This person had also failed to qualify to be at the helm, and it turned out that he often was lost on the navigation map. My buddy and I, who were qualified, tried to improve this person's capabilities but gave up by the time we were in the Mediterranean. We both went on twelve hour shifts.

I don't remember much about the visit to Portsmouth except the constant cycle of providing rides to a host of people.

There was a tour of London which is also a bit fuzzy, but my stomach remembers Fish and Chips, my eyes remember walking through the London Art Museum and driving by Big Ben.

We hosted many dignitaries and their families and gave them rides.

Once we had given all the dignitaries rides we departed for Brest France. Once again the entire visit was spent on giving rides to dignitaries and their families. Other than the repetitive nature of giving the rides, it was an easy time.

We visited Brest because it was the location of the French Naval Academy that was established in 1830. It became one of the largest naval bases and now houses the Brest Naval Training Center.

It was in Brest that I enjoyed Courvoisier brandy, the Original Napoleon Cognac. I was shocked to learn that that a shot of the brandy went for twenty-five cents, but a Coke sold for a dollar. Later I would be shocked again by the fact that the price for the exact sized drink in Washington DC was forty times more expensive.

Then it was time to fly through the Strait of Gibraltar and on to Toulan, France. The Rock of Gibraltar and a North African peak together form the "Pillars of Hercules" that were said to have been placed there to by Hercules to celebrate his success of seizing the cattle of the three bodied giant, Geryon. There is fourteen miles between the two at the closest point. We flew by the Rock of Gibraltar and then took a turn to the south until we caught sight of Mount Hacho. We flew along the coast of Morocco and Algeria and then turned north toward the coast of Spain. In both cases we were flying in view of the coast and the crew was out on the deck enjoying the scenery.

Think of the journey to Toulon as driving across the US from west coast to east coast at fifty miles an hour. There was plenty of time to take in the beauty of the Mediterranean area. Our navigation maps were up to date so the only thing we had to do was to pay attention and fly on a clean route. It was interesting to learn that the Mediterranean is divided into different seas. The Alboran Sea is immediately after the Strait of Gibraltar, we then flew the Balearic Sea as we passed by Barcelona and finally we flying in the Ligurian Sea. All I can say it was all the Mediterranean to me.

Toulon consisted of additional touring of dignitaries. Quiet evenings enjoying the French Cuisine was the evening activity and a bicycle ride was the activity on a day off. Nothing stands out in my memory about the time there. The Time there was short and then we went on to Italy.

Ron Mueller

Chapter 7: Italy, Greece, Turkey

Our arrival at La Spezia was greeted with fanfare and a small band. While there we were treated to several dinners. We did daily tour runs for several days.

Then we worked with the designers who were working on the design of a Italian hydrofoil similar to the Tucumcari. They were interested in the performance of the Tucumcari under several different scenarios. We demonstrated the use of the 40 mm gun by firing it at targets. We also demonstrated the use of the fifty caliber machine guns and the 81mm mortar.

It was interesting to listen to the designers and I enjoyed reviewing the control logic for the foils they were designing and shared how I had to tune the Tucumcari's foil control system for the period of the sea or ocean waves. The tunning was something that I had added to the original Boeing capability by installing variable resistors and capacitors. This slight modification allowed me to tweak the stability performance.

I learned that the shorter and steeper the wavelength the lower the performance of the Tucumcari became. The longer wave lengths were the most forgiving. The Tucumcari was originally designed for the longer Pacific wavelength.

I am not sure whether the Italian hydrofoils were ever built.

Before we left La Spezia, we were all award an Italian Service metal for providing guidance to their hydrofoil program. So, I am a holder of an Italian medal!

We left La Spezia on the way to Amalfi where we were going to spend a day to split up the transit along the coast of Italy. This was another time where our third navigator demonstrated his lack of navigating capability. I went down to lunch and left him on the watch as the navigator. When I came back later I asked him to share the location of the Tucumcari. He pointed to the map, and I immediately knew that he was totally lost. I relieved him and told him to go to lunch. I used the radar and the land radio signals and quickly had the location. He had hardly moved more than ten miles; the boat was seventy mile farther along.

Amalfi was a pleasant stop where we did not have any duties to fulfill. We were there for one day. Then we were off to Naples. Where we did provide some rides to a variety of dignitaries.

I have several good memories of Naples.

US Navy-A Footprint in My Life

One was of a bike ride that I had decided on. It was along a narrow mountain ridge road that provided a scenic via of Naples. I was riding along when a panel truck honked and came zooming up behind me. I moved to the very edge of the road and as the truck went by I slid down the hill. I was laying on my back, holding on to my bike hoping that I did not slide down the slope that was close to being a cliff. I pulled myself back up to the road. I was wondering whether to turn back when I saw a small stand just ahead. It was offering a variety of refreshments to sell. I only remember ordering a lemonade and watching it being made. The glass was filled about one third with sugar, then the lemon was squeezed in, and the sparkling water poured in. No ice, but it tasted great.

I decided to continue on my ride. Then I came to a house that had an open porch overlooking the Mediterranean that was also a restaurant. I remember enjoying one of the best pizza's that I have ever had. It was thin crusted, had a variety of clams, sardines, fish, tomatoes and was drizzled in olive oil. It had a delicious flavor very different from other pizza's I had enjoyed and a flavor that I have never experienced since.

I ended the day exhausted from my ride, but I knew that I had experienced one of my more exciting rides.

The other memory of Naples is that of going to Pompei. I prepared myself by buying a bottle of Italian wine, I think Chianti, a Baquet, some cheese, and slices of sausage. My intension was to find myself a scenic and shady place and have lunch at the ruins and then take a tour. I don't remember the details about the tour itself, but I remember sitting and looking into the ruins and enjoying my sandwich and talking with a young woman who was also sitting in the shade and having her lunch. I don't really remember her after all this time other than the fact that it turned out to be a very relaxing conversation and enjoyable tour.

The next part of the journey took us between the tip of the boot and Sicilia around the bottom of the boot to Brindisi. The port there was a cesspool. We docked and decided to protect the water turbines from the water by blocking the water intakes. I was the one to go do it. I made sure my wet suit was soaked with fresh clean water. I wore head gear as well and went under with two wooden plugs that were about a foot in diameter. I had to wear a lead weight belt to enable me to sink so I could get to the intakes. I put the plugs in and once I was clear each turbine was fired so that the wooden plugs were pulled in place. Then I was pulled up and hosed off. I took a nice long shower. Meanwhile fresh water was pumped through the engines to clean them.

We stayed in Brindisi only a few days. I don't recall doing anything but doing some touring and enjoying a dinner there.

US Navy-A Footprint in My Life

We left the port using our diesel engine and once we were out to clean water, I went under the boat and removed the plugs.

Then we began our flight to Athens.

Along the way we came across a Russian destroyer sitting idly out in the sea. We decided to get a closer look and took the Tucumcari on a flight around it. During the flight around it we noticed that the guns were rotating around with us. We decided it was time to hightail it. We gave them three wags as we flew on. I wonder to this day what had transpired on the Russian ship.

Athens was a unique experience. I took a tour of the Acropolis and around the hilltop citadel and ancient buildings like the colonnaded Parthenon temple.

As usual, we gave rides to the Greek dignitaries.

The most memorable time in Athens was going to an all-night wine festival. The festival was in a large park that had a walkway wandering through it. There was an entrance fee but then all the wine you could drink was free. The food that was available had to be paid for. I made sure that I ate well then began to taste every wine that was offered. I took only one sip of most wines and then walked to the next offering. I began around eight at night and ended up at the other end of the park by about three in the morning. I was feeling fine. I noticed that there were several of the Wood County sailors that were passed out at the exit. I flagged down a cab and made a deal with him to take all the extra sailors as well. Together we piled the sailors in the back seat, and I got into the front seat.

Luckily, he was able to deposit us at the end to the pier where the Wood County was docked. The sailors were still passed out. I went to the ship and arranged with the night watch to let me carry the sailors on board. They went for a coffee in the mess, and I carried the sailors down into the bunking area of the ship.

The effort to bring them on board made me sick. I ended up in the latrine area where I got sick. I then took a long shower and went to my bunk to sleep it off. I never received any thanks for saving those sailors butts.

They would have faced a Captains mast if they had not made it back on board. I doubt they even recalled what had happened. Had I left them in the park they would most likely have been found stripped of their clothes.

Then it was time to go to Turkey and the last stop at Gölcük.

The flight there was one that provided the Tucumcari and the rest of us an experience that is hard to forget. A raging storm came directly at us. We had to stop flying and use just our diesel propulsion. The oncoming waves would sweep over us, and we would bob out on the other side. We had to close the turbine air intakes so that we would not take on water. For several days, I don't recall exactly how many Tucumcari went backwards. The entire crew was seasick from the violent swaying action. I am sure that the wing struts that went down ten feet into the water was the only thing that saved us. We went backward while our engine was trying to move us forward a five knot speed.

Once the storm passed, we were able to fly on. The Wood County was docked, and we joined her.

Once again we gave rides to dignitaries.

The unique memory was driving from the ship to a restaurant where we were going to be thanked for providing the rides. On the way out and again on the way back into the area where we were docked, I got to look down the barrel of an AK47 as the guards on each side of the car checked our identification. I learned later that some sort of rebellion was under way. We had a lead and rear armored car that escorted us. The car driver pointed out the guard towers that had machine guns that were located along the highway. I have no recollection of the dinner or any of the people at the dinner except for my shipmates.

Then it was time to return to the US. The Tucumcari was loaded onto the Wood County and the return trip to the US took place. This time period must have been fairly dull because I do not recall it at all.

My next memories are about getting transferred off of the Tucumcari and assigned to the Wood County.

Ron Mueller

Chapter 8: Captain Mueller!

The transfer to the Wood County came as a surprise. Only two of us from the Tucumcari were transferred to it.

Somehow my transfer paperwork got lost or misplaced. I ended up going to Washington to get it cleared up. My friend who had transferred to the Wood County came with me. While there we went to an upscale restaurant for dinner. It was after dinner; I think I did lamb chops. We paid for dinner and went to the bar where I ordered a shot of Courvoisier for each of us. Then when I paid for it I was shocked to learn that each of the shots cost almost eight dollars. This was the same brand that in France I had paid less than a dollar.

My transfer paperwork was found. It had been misfiled. By personally coming to find it I had expedited getting it found.

Soon after getting the transfer and beginning to lead the Electronics shop, I learned that the Wood County was to be decommissioned.

Not long after and before decommissioning started there was a race riot on the ship. One of the electronic team members in my command was black. He was great guy and he and the rest of the black sailors had barricaded themselves in one of the troop carrying areas.

The Captain and a team working with him was getting ready to cut through the bulkhead and arrest the black sailors.

I told the Captain that I thought that I could get them to come out.

I went the bulkhead door and was able to convince the sailors inside to let me come in. Once in I wondered if I had made a mistake because I had a knife at my throat. The sailor from my crew got the knife removed. I asked them what had happened. They explained that one of the white boatswain mates had started a fight. The fight had escalated. It was clear that they were in the minority and had all retreated and locked themselves in to protect themselves.

I let them know that I was going to go out and talk with the Captain and see about getting the situation resolved in a fair way.

In my discussion with the Captain, I clarified the situation and suggested that every one of the crew take racial sensitivity training. He liked that idea since it diffused the immediate situation and put him a positive light.

It was clear that my action had put me in good favor with the Captain.

US Navy-A Footprint in My Life

Not long after we were all assigned to a barracks on the base. I was given the responsibility for the managing the barracks with a small team to keep order. I had a private room and a small refrigerator. I was soon in the business of selling Boon's Farm Apple wine. I would have the wine in the fridge and sell the bottles at a low but profitable price to anyone desiring a bottle. After my initial investment, the wine business was self-sustaining.

The decommissioning job of the Electronics team was to prepare all the electronics to be stowed away and all the areas that we used was to be stripped of the insulation and then the walls and flooring were to be cleaned and painted with red lead.

I organized my crew so that each day we had a specific area to do and that as soon as that area was done we would leave the ship. We set a record in getting our stuff done.

The most harrowing thing that I did was to crawl out on the beam at the top of the mast to take down the electronic gear. I was hanging on for dear life as I unbolted the gear and lowered it down.

Once we were complete, the Captain asked me to take on a few more members and help get some of the ballast tanks cleaned, dried and red leaded. This proved to be a challenge. I had a mixed group. A few members were junior officers, and the others were just additional sailors.

I followed the same routine of setting up the day's cleaning goal and letting them know that when the day's goal was reached everyone got to go on their way.

The first obstacle that I faced was the refusal of the junior officers to help in cleaning the designated area. I said that they could just sit in the middle of the area to be cleaned. When the water hoses came on and the water hit the walls they got soaked. That seemed to get them to be willing to participate. We got done in record time and a I had a team willing to follow my lead.

We got reassigned to the ballast area. This was a space that we all had to bend over to get in. This time I had a few new group members added to my previous group. The new group members were mostly troublemakers from other groups. The Captain asked me to get them to work.

When we got into the ballast area, I had one of my previous crew members close the hatch to the point no one could get out. I pointed out the area that needed to get done and explained the process that we would follow. The troublemakers refused to participate. My other team members knew the routine. They turned on the hoses and began to clean the area. After the troublemakers realized that they were getting totally soaked and that they could not get out they relented and began to help. Within a day they were as willing to work as the rest of the team. They were now getting off early while the teams they had been on were still working.

US Navy-A Footprint in My Life

Once again we got done in record time and I was asked to move the team into the engine room and help prepare the engine room and the engines for mothballing. The engine preparation would be handled by the engine room crew but the water and gunk around the engine needed to be cleaned out.

I looked around and was trying to come up with an idea to motivate a tired team. I saw the engine room crew getting ready to wheel out several large toolboxes. I asked what they were going to do with them. They shared that the tools and toolboxes would be thrown into one of the dumpsters on the pier.

I asked them to hold off and went to the Captain to clear the idea I had. He supported my idea. I had my team randomly throw the tools into the water around the engines. As the water was pumped out, and the structural areas cleaned any tool a person found was theirs. To this day, I have the tools that I found.

The engine room was once again cleaned in record time.

The crews I led ended up preparing almost a twenty percent of the Wood County.

Everyone ended the decommissioning preparation in an exhausted state.

The Captain had tried to get me to re-enlist and go into the NESEP program (by that time they had started to accept people with my eyesight). I thanked him and let him know that I desired to get out and go to college on my own.

I had been in a little over five years. I knew that I wanted to get out. The favor I asked for was an early out that let me start at a University in its normal school cycle.

I was surprised to learn that I had been named acting Captain during the final moth balling preparation and upon completion, I would be released from the service.

What a nice departure gift.

The Ship went into the final preparation in the Philadelphia Navy Yard. I set up the team that was assigned so that we operated on a southern swing shift that provided each of us with a four day weekend every month. This went on during the summer and by August I had my early out.

The next phase of my journey had me in Pensacola Junior College.

I was to find a treasure there and eventually would reap the benefits beyond what I had imagined for myself.

I remained in the Naval Reserve because it provided me with a small income. My final military release date was August 8, 1976.

The End

US Navy-A Footprint in My Life

About the Author

Ronald E. Mueller
remwriter95@gmail.com
Ron grew up in what is now Flint River State Park in Southeast Iowa. The 170-year-old house Ron lived in is built into a hillside. It faces a 125-foot-high cliff towering over the little Flint River. The house and the land talked to him about; the passing of time, the struggle to conquer the land, the struggles people faced and the wonder of nature.

He climbed the cliffs, crawled into the caves, dove from the swimming rock, collected clams from the bottom of the pond, gigged and skinned frogs for their legs. He trapped muskrats for fur, hunted raccoon in the dead of night, and with only a stick hunted rabbits in the dead of winter.

His young life was outdoors, and nature tested him.

He walked to a one room stone schoolhouse uphill both ways. A stern but warm-hearted teacher, Mrs. Henry was instrumental in shaping his character as she shepherded him from the fourth to the eighth grade. A Montessori before its time. It was a great way to grow up.

His experiences inter-twined with snippets of fantasy lend themselves to the adventures he leads the reader through.

Ron Mueller

Published by: Around the World Publishing LLC.

QR Links to
ATWP.US web site

Printed in the USA
CPSIA information can be obtained
at www.ICGtesting.com
LVHW010336260923
759112LV00062B/1193